Building Peace

A Pastoral Reflection on the Response to
The Challenge of Peace
National Conference of Catholic Bishops

A Report

on *The Challenge of Peace* and
Policy Developments 1983-1988
Ad Hoc Committee on the Moral Evaluation
of Deterrence

National Conference of Catholic Bishops
June 1988

Following the November 1985 general meeting of the National Conference of Catholic Bishops, an ad hoc committee of bishops was appointed to assess whether the conditions for the moral acceptability of deterrence, which were set forth in the 1983 pastoral letter, *The Challenge of Peace: God's Promise and Our Response,* were being met. The ad hoc committee submitted to the bishops the first draft of a pastoral reflection and a report in April 1988. Approval of the pastoral reflection and the committee report was given during the plenary assembly in Collegeville, Minnesota in June 1988. Accordingly, publication of this pastoral reflection, *Building Peace: A Pastoral Reflection on the Response to "The Challenge of Peace,"* and this report of the ad hoc committee, *A Report on "The Challenge of Peace" and Policy Developments 1983-1988,* are authorized by the undersigned.

Monsignor Daniel F. Hoye
General Secretary
NCCB/USCC

July 7, 1988

Contents

A Pastoral Reflection on the Response to
The Challenge of Peace
  Introduction / 3
  The Response Was Extraordinary / 4
  The Continuing Challenge / 5
  The Deterrence Report / 7
  Becoming a Peacemaking Church / 7
  Conclusions / 11

A Report on *The Challenge of Peace* **and**
Policy Developments 1983-1988
  Introduction / 15
    A. The Moral Meaning of the Nuclear Age / 15
    B. The Church and the Nuclear Age / 20
    C. The U.S. Bishops and the Nuclear
        Dilemma / 23
    D. The Significance of the Present Moment / 27
  I. *The Challenge of Peace*: A Summary
  Statement / 29
    A. Use of Nuclear Weapons / 31
    B. The Strategy of Deterrence / 35
    C. Criteria and Conditions for Policy
        Evaluation / 39
  II. Policy Developments: Assessment and
  Recommendations / 43
    A. Arms Control Policy / 43
      1. The INF Treaty / 45
      2. The Nuclear and Space Talks (NST) / 46
      3. Existing Treaties / 47
      4. New Deployments / 47
      5. Independent Initiatives / 48
      6. Conventional Arms Control / 48

7. Nuclear Non-proliferation / 51

B. Technological Developments / 55

   1. SDI: What Is It? / 57

   2. SDI: Technology, Strategy and
     Arms Control / 62

   3. SDI: The Moral Argument / 67

C. The Economy and Military Spending / 73

III. The Status of Deterrence: An Evaluation / 76

Building Peace

A Pastoral Reflection on the Response to
The Challenge of Peace

For her part, the Church recognizes her responsibility in building peace. Not only does she recall the principles drawn from the Gospel, but she also seeks to form people capable of being true artisans of peace in the places where they live.[1]

John Paul II

Introduction

1.   Five years ago, we bishops of the United States adopted our pastoral letter on nuclear arms, *The Challenge of Peace.* As pastors, we sought to say a word of hope in a time of fear, to challenge believers to become artisans of peace in the nuclear age. As teachers, we sought to share the Church's wisdom on nuclear arms and apply it in one of the world's nuclear superpowers. We shared both the complexity and urgency of these matters, calling for prayer, reflection and action to reduce the moral and physical dangers of the nuclear age.

2.   Five years later, we offer this brief reflection on how *The Challenge of Peace* has challenged our Church. We also offer it as an introduction to the report of the Ad Hoc Committee on the Moral Evaluation of Deterrence. We look back with gratitude to the efforts to share the letter and we look ahead with commitment to the continuing

---

[1] Pope John Paul II, "Address to Diplomatic Corps" (Rome, January 9, 1988), *L'Osservatore Romano,* English weekly edition (January 25, 1988): no. 12, p. 8.

challenge of building peace in a world still threatened by nuclear arms.

The Response Was Extraordinary

3. When we began to write our letter, we had no idea of the attention and activity it would generate. Among the bishops of the United States, we found great concern and consensus. Our efforts within the bishops' conference to articulate and apply the Church's teaching on nuclear arms gave rise to considerable debate and remarkable unity in our common efforts to share the gospel message of peace and justice.

4. In dioceses and parishes, the letter launched an unprecedented process of prayer, preaching, education, reflection, discussion and action. Countless Catholics have gathered in conferences and workshops, in homes and parishes to pray for peace and to reflect on the challenges of the letter.

5. In many of our own schools, colleges and universities the message of the letter has been integrated into courses, conferences and curricula. In secular colleges and universities, in research institutes and in the specialized literature on nuclear issues, *The Challenge of Peace* is used on a frequent basis.

6. In terms of the broader public debate and decision making on nuclear policy, the pastoral letter has been both a catalyst and a resource in the discussion of the moral dimensions of nuclear arms and strategy. We have learned from and been strengthened by the efforts of other religious groups who have developed and shared their own reflections on the moral dimensions of nuclear arms.

7. *The Challenge of Peace* has strengthened our Church, enriched its life and engaged many of its people. But too many still remain unaware of the letter and the teaching of the Church in this area. Much more needs to be done to share the gospel message of peace founded on justice and to bring this message more clearly into the public arena. We know we have a long way to go, but we are grateful and encouraged by the significant activity that emerged as a result of the pastoral letter. We hope these brief reflections will give new impetus to efforts to share the letter and act on its implications.

The Continuing Challenge

8.   The peace pastoral was not some passing preoccupation or brief phase in the Church's life. It represents an ongoing commitment to weave concern for these matters into the fabric of Catholic life. As the letter said: "Peacemaking is not an optional commitment. It is a requirement of our faith. We are called to be peacemakers, not by some movement of the moment, but by our Lord Jesus."[2]

9.   Nuclear policy remains a central moral dilemma for believers. We still live in a world torn by divisions and threatened by the nuclear arsenals of East and West. In our 1986 pastoral letter, *Economic Justice for All,* we reiterated our concern that the extraordinary amount of resources allocated to

---

[2] National Conference of Catholic Bishops, *The Challenge of Peace: God's Promise and Our Response* (Washington, D.C.: USCC Office of Publishing and Promotion Services, 1983), no. 333.

arms were depriving our society of the resources necessary to meet the just needs of the poor. As Pope John Paul II said in January of 1988: "The stockpiling of these weapons in itself constitutes a threat to peace, as well as a provocation to the peoples that lack the essentials for survival and development."[3] In his powerful encyclical, *On Social Concern (Sollicitudo Rei Socialis)*, the Holy Father pointed out that the rivalry between the superpowers, the arms trade and the worldwide investment in weapons of war have disastrous effects on the lives of the poor in the developing countries.[4]

10. We stand at a moment of genuine crisis and unavoidable choices. The fate of the human family, perhaps even of the earth itself, may well depend upon the choices made in the months and years ahead. As human beings, we cannot be indifferent to this crisis. As American citizens, we have the freedom and responsibility to influence our own nation's policies. As Catholics, we are called to be peacemakers shaped by our traditional teaching on nuclear arms.

---

[3] Pope John Paul II, "Address to Diplomatic Corps," no. 3, p. 6.

[4] Pope John Paul II, *On Social Concern (Sollicitudo Rei Socialis)* (Washington, D.C. : USCC Office of Publishing and Promotion Services, 1988), nos. 20-24.

The Deterrence Report

11. *A Report on "The Challenge of Peace" and Policy Developments 1983-1988* seeks to assess the facts of the nuclear problem in 1988 in light of the principles of our pastoral letter. We believe it faithfully reflects and applies Catholic teaching on nuclear arms. In our report, we renew the judgment of the pastoral letter that we can offer only "strictly conditioned moral acceptance" of nuclear deterrence. We cannot simply condemn or embrace deterrence. Rather, we call for urgent and persistent efforts to move more decisively toward effective arms control and mutual disarmament, to fashion a more secure and lasting basis for peace and to put in place nuclear policies which reflect more clearly the moral principles and values of *The Challenge of Peace.* This report will guide the efforts of our conference in this area and will strengthen our work for effective arms control, mutual disarmament and genuine peace in our divided world. We hope Catholics and all those of goodwill will read it, reflect upon its basic principles and prudential judgments and act on its call to shape policies to reduce the moral and physical dangers of this nuclear age.

Becoming a Peacemaking Church

12. As pastors and believers, we are required by the Gospel to do far more than to develop a pastoral letter and initiate efforts to begin to educate and act on the Church's teaching. We also need to do more than to assess current developments for

their moral implications. We must work to broaden, deepen and strengthen the Church's work for peace. The whole Church is called to become a *peacemaking church,* to "form people capable of being true artisans of peace," in the words of Pope John Paul II.[5] In this task, we are united with our Holy Father and the Universal Church. It was in Coventry that Pope John Paul said: "Like a cathedral, peace must be constructed patiently and with unshakable faith."[6] Five years after the adoption of our letter, we recommit ourselves to that task. We are called to seek practical ways to make the peace and justice of the Kingdom more visible in a world torn by fear, hatred and violence.

13. A *peacemaking church* needs to constantly pray for peace. As we share God's word and celebrate the Eucharist, there will be many opportunities to reflect and pray on the biblical basis for peacemaking and church teaching on nuclear arms. Every worshiping community should regularly include the cause of peace in its prayers of petition. It is in prayer that we encounter Jesus who is our peace and learn from him the way to peace. It is in prayer we find the hope and perseverance which sustain us as instruments of Christ's peace in the world. In this Marian year, we call on Mary, the Queen of Peace, to intercede for us and for the people of the world that we may walk in the ways of peace.

14. A *church of peacemaking* is also a community which regularly shares the Church's teaching on peace in its schools, religious education efforts and

---

[5] Pope John Paul II, "Address to Diplomatic Corps," no. 12, p. 8.

[6] Pope John Paul II, "Homily at Bagington Airport" (Conventry, May 30, 1982), *Origins* 12:4 (June 10, 1982): p. 55, cited in *The Challenge of Peace,* no. 200.

other parish activities. A special effort is necessary in our institutions of higher education where research, teaching and scholarship can be put at the service of peace. Much has been done to integrate fully and faithfully the Church's teaching in our educational efforts. We urge that the teaching of the letter be presented in its totality, including the principles governing a nation's right and obligation of self-defense and an individual's right of conscientious objection.

15. Much more needs to be done to integrate fully the Church's teaching in our educational efforts. We especially need to work toward a more fully developed theology of peace. As the pastoral letter said: "A theology of peace should ground the task of peacemaking solidly in the biblical vision of the Kingdom of God, then place it centrally in the ministry of the Church."[7] We need continued theological reflection in colleges, universities, seminaries and other centers of thought and learning on peacemaking, on the complex question of deterrence and on how the Church can provide clear teaching and strong witness for peace grounded in our Christian faith.

16. A *church of peacemaking* is a community which speaks and acts for peace, a community which consistently raises fundamental moral questions about the policies that guide the arsenals of the world. As believers and citizens, we are called to use our voices and votes to support effective efforts to reverse the arms race and move toward genuine peace with justice. The Deterrence Report focuses on the ethical dimensions of nuclear issues. Our conference will be actively sharing these principles and policy directions with those who shape

---

[7] *The Challenge of Peace,* no. 25.

the policies of our nation as part of our continuing commitment to defend human life whenever it is threatened. The U.S. Catholic Conference and our Department of Social Development and World Peace have a special responsibility in this area, but it is also a task for the whole Church. Each of us is called to participate in the debate over how our nation and world can best move toward mutual disarmament and genuine peace with justice.

17. We serve a diverse Church with legitimate differences on how best to apply principles to policies. The pastoral and other church teaching are best shared in respectful dialogue. The voice of a *peacemaking church* must reflect the facts, rest on competent analysis and understand that persons of goodwill sometimes differ on specific questions. We cannot just proclaim positions. We must argue our case for peace, not only with conviction and competence, but also with civility and charity. We need to bring special pastoral skill and sensitivity to the important task of helping our people become builders of peace in their own situations. For many of our people, these are personal and professional concerns as well as public issues. They deserve personal support and creative pastoral care as they try to live the values of the Gospel in their own demanding roles and responsibilities and as they wrestle with the ethical dimensions of their own work and citizenship.

18. Finally, a *peacemaking church* is a community which keeps hope alive. We sometimes find ourselves suspended between hope and fear. Surrounded by weapons of mass destruction, we try to imagine and to bring about a future without them. Our faith does not insulate us from problems; it calls us to confront them and to a constant effort to

build a better, more lasting basis for peace, knowing that God's grace will never fail us.

Conclusions

19. Five years after our letter, we are still at a beginning, not an end. We are grateful for all that has been done to share the message of the letter. We affirm the efforts to act faithfully on its implications. We call for a renewed commitment to pray, educate and work for peace at every level of the Church's life.

20. We pray that the leaders of our nation and world will find the wisdom, the will and the ways to move toward genuine peace and mutual disarmament. We pray that believers will become more effective witnesses and workers for peace, helping our world say "no" to the violence of war, "no" to nuclear destruction, "no" to an arms race that robs the poor and endangers us all.

21. As bishops, we recommit ourselves to our pastoral letter of five years ago and to the task of sharing and acting on its message. Our commitment to this task cannot be diminished by the passage of time, the press of other priorities or the frustrations of the moment. Now is a time to build on the activities of the past five years, to renew our efforts to educate and advocate for peace, to help make our Church a truly peacemaking community and to work with all people of goodwill to help shape a world of peace and justice.

22. In renewing this commitment, we must remember who calls us to this task and why. It was Jesus who said: "Blessed are the peacemakers, for

they will be called children of God" (Matthew 5:9). As his followers, we take up again the urgent and continuing priority of "building peace" in the nuclear age.[8]

---

[8] Pope John Paul II, "Address to Diplomatic Corps," no. 12, p. 8.

A Report

on *The Challenge of Peace* and
Policy Developments 1983-1988

Introduction

1. *The Challenge of Peace*[1] was the product of many influences and many ideas. No single resource was more evident in the document than the teaching of Pope John Paul II; the basic theme of the pastoral letter was an effort to develop the Holy Father's statement at Hiroshima in 1981: "From now on it is only through a conscious choice and through a deliberate policy that humanity can survive."[2]

A. The Moral Meaning of the Nuclear Age

2. The pastoral letter of 1983 sought to define the moral choices of the nuclear age. Using religious, moral, political and strategic ideas, *The Challenge of Peace* analyzed the political context and the strategic content of the policy choices and the personal choices of conscience which stand before nations and citizens in the nuclear age. The document was the product of the Catholic religious-moral tradition, but it was addressed to both the community of the Church and the wider civil community. Part of the content of the pastoral letter was a statement of religious values and

---

[1] National Conference of Catholic Bishops, *The Challenge of Peace: God's Promise and Our Response* (Washington, D.C.: USCC Office of Publishing and Promotion Services, 1983).

[2] John Paul II, "Address to Scientists and Scholars" (Hiroshima, February 25, 1981), *Origins* 10:39 (March 12, 1981): no. 4, p. 621.

moral principles which are not limited by time or changing conditions. Other parts of the letter involved descriptions of problems and proposals for policy which were contingent in nature and in need of continuing revision. A basic moral judgment of *The Challenge of Peace,* a "strictly conditioned moral acceptance" of deterrence, requires a continuing political-moral analysis of the elements of deterrence policy as that policy is defined and implemented by the United States and the Soviet Union.

3. In order to contribute to this necessary moral analysis, the general meeting of the NCCB/USCC voted in November 1985 to commission an explicit public review of how the "conditions" of *The Challenge of Peace* were being observed in the nuclear arms competition. Following this action Bishop James Malone, then president of NCCB/USCC, appointed this ad hoc committee and gave it the following mandate:

> The basis of the study will be the moral principles and the moral judgments of the pastoral letter. The task of the committee will be to assess all the relevant [facts] and moral principles needed to present to the NCCB membership a judgment on the moral status of deterrence.[3]

4. This *Report on "The Challenge of Peace" and Policy Developments 1983-1988* is a logical extension of the position the National Conference of Catholic Bishops adopted in the pastoral letter. In writing this report, we presuppose the biblical, theological and moral teaching of *The Challenge*

---

[3]NCCB Ad Hoc Committee on the Moral Evaluation of Deterrence, *Origins* 15:24 (November 28, 1985): p. 400.

of Peace; our task is to assess a series of events, policy choices and technical trends not fully explored in the pastoral letter. We write this report to remain faithful to our own commitment of 1983, and because of the continuing urgency of the situation posed by nuclear weapons for our nation, for other nations and for the global community.

5. The moral dimension of the problem created by nuclear weapons cannot be understood solely in terms of the weapons themselves. It is the political context in which nuclear weapons exist, joined with the technological nature of the weaponry, which creates the qualitatively new issues of the nuclear age. Essentially, the nuclear age has been shaped by a quantum leap in the development of military arsenals and no corresponding change in our form of political organization. Politically, the world is a community of independent sovereign states each of which retains the capability of resorting to force to resolve political, territorial and economic disputes. Hence, in this political configuration the perennial problems which have faced states for centuries persist:

- how to prevent aggression,
- how to shape relationships on the basis of justice and freedom,
- how to protect human rights within states and among states,
- how to protect the small states from designs of larger nations.

6. These questions, in their empirical and ethical dimensions, are the classical issues of international politics. It is because of these questions that states with differing ideologies and competing interests contend with each other daily and all too frequently clash militarily. This century has

witnessed two wars of global dimensions. Since the end of the Second World War, there have been over 150 recorded military conflicts. Quite apart from the existence of nuclear weapons, the classical problems of war and peace are still with us. The first goal of politics and morality should be to avoid all resort to force as a means of settling differences. But we do not live apart from nuclear weapons; they exist and they have changed radically the way the classical questions are understood.

7. The moral problem of the nuclear age arises when the classical political questions are joined to the contemporary technological prospects of a nuclear war. There is a moral mandate to protect the values of justice, freedom and order in the international arena. There is an absolute moral norm which protects the right to life of innocent persons. There is also a moral imperative to avoid nuclear war or anything which could lead toward or increase the possibility of nuclear conflict. The moral problem of the nuclear age is how to keep the peace and how to ensure that it is a just peace, one which preserves the freedom of nations, their right to development and the human rights of persons.

8. The particular theme which *The Challenge of Peace* focused upon and to which we return in this report is the unique dangers posed by the nuclear arsenals. The uniqueness arises from the scope and degree of devastation these weapons can wreak. In the nuclear debate of the 1980s the kind of destruction which the arsenals of the superpowers can cause has been brought home to the public with new urgency and great specificity. Rather than repeat these statistics and predictions here, it is more pertinent to state the widely shared conclusion which flows from an understanding of

the meaning of nuclear war. Nuclear war remains a possibility, but it is increasingly seen as devoid of the rational political purpose and moral limits which have made war a justifiable activity in the past. Nuclear weapons threaten to destroy the very objectives which once provided the political and moral justification for using force. To state the case in the categories of our pastoral letter: Traditional just-war theory requires that just causes exist for nations to assert a right of self-defense or defense of others, but nuclear war challenges the basic idea of what constitutes a just means. Reason, morality and faith combine today in opposition to the idea that nuclear war fits our traditional understanding of justifiable use of force.

9. It is easier to draw this conclusion than it is to pursue its consequences. For living in the nuclear age means that we can condemn nuclear war, but we will still have to live with nuclear weapons. There are several dimensions to the nuclear dilemma:

- *the scientific community* unlocked the mystery of nuclear power--we will never return to an age when the knowledge of how to build nuclear weapons is absent;
- *military strategists* are commanded to prepare for nuclear war, but to do so in a fashion which reduces the possibilities that it will ever occur;
- *political leaders* threaten to resort to nuclear weapons if necessary, and simultaneously proclaim that their use is unthinkable;
- *the general public* fluctuates between moments of great fear of nuclear holocaust, great hope that negotiations will solve the nuclear dilemma and the

normal instinct of suppressing any thought about this perplexing and frightening reality.

10. How do we live with nuclear weapons, politically, strategically and morally, until the day when we can live without them? Some believe such a day is a distinct possibility; others are equally convinced such a goal is a delusion or at least a dangerous distraction from more modest objectives of living with nuclear weapons more safely. In *The Challenge of Peace*, we held out the hope of a world freed of the nuclear threat, but we addressed in much greater detail the issues of how to move toward a world with less nuclear danger and greater political control and how to maintain a clear sense of the moral imperatives which are older than the nuclear age and must be related to it.

11. This report is designed to continue the quest for a world rid of the nuclear danger and to continue the process of defining the political and moral direction which should guide national policy and personal choice in the nuclear age.

B. The Church and the Nuclear Age

12. It will take the wisdom and courage of many individuals and institutions to dispel the nuclear paradox: scientists and strategists, politicians and poets, citizens and educators. The Catholic Church is called by its own doctrine--by the Gospel of Christ and the tradition of the centuries--to be a participant in the pursuit of peace.

13. The papal teaching of the nuclear age, from Pius XII to John Paul II, has been the leading voice in the Church, seeking to adapt and to apply the

classical moral teaching on war to the dramatically new situation created by weapons of mass destruction. The papal teaching has been consistently realistic about the problems of peace, but it has been insistently prophetic in its assertion that a "moral aboutface" is needed to make progress toward disarmament. Other voices in the Church, from episcopal conferences to organized efforts among laity and religious have responded to papal leadership and the call of Vatican II to face this "moment of supreme crisis" in which we live. The complexity of the crisis assures a diversity of views within the Church about the best means to address it. But the moral tradition of the Church establishes a set of common values to guide our efforts.

14.   The principal value threatened by the nuclear age is one which stands at the center of the Church's ministry of peace: the defense of human life. Each life is sacred and all life is a gift from God. The resources of our faith, the Sacred Scriptures and Catholic tradition, teach us that we are entrusted with life--we neither own it nor control it; human life is sacred because it originates with God and because we are destined for eternal communion with God. Each person carries his or her life as a sacred trust, and we believe that the lives of others are to be treated with awe and reverence. Respect for human life as sacred is at the core of Catholic moral doctrine. In this century the sacredness of human life has been violated by totalitarian political systems of left and right and by the scourge of war at the global and local level. In our time the paradoxical fact is that life is sometimes threatened by discoveries which attest to the genius of the human spirit, but which stand in need of moral guidance. This has been the case

since the beginning of the nuclear age. Unlocking the power of atomic energy was a unique watershed in human history; yet its development as an instrument of warfare poses an unprecedented threat to human welfare. Pope John Paul II repeatedly has placed his moral teaching on the nuclear age in this broad context of the relationship of technology, politics and ethics. The challenge of the nuclear age, according to the Holy Father, is not to condemn scientific discovery nor the technology which flows from it, but to develop the moral vision and political wisdom to set a direction for and place restraints upon the power placed in human hands by splitting the atom.

15. Protecting human life from nuclear destruction must be pursued in tandem with promoting those values necessary for life to be lived with dignity. Pope John XXIII in *Pacem in Terris* set forth the values in which national and international society must be built: truth, justice, freedom and love. A lasting peace must reside in these values; sometimes peace requires the use of force, domestically or internationally, to defend these values. But the challenge of the nuclear age is to protect life, promote basic values and prevent recourse to nuclear weapons in any form.

16. Catholic teaching on war and peace has a positive conception of peace. It is not simply the absence of violence, but the product of an order built into human relationships at every level of life. Peace is the fruit of order; a morally justified social order is shaped by truth, justice, freedom and love. The paradox of the nuclear age is that vast amounts of intellectual and political energy must be expended to assure that something does not occur: nuclear war. But this is an insufficient conception of the political-moral challenge of our time. An equal

amount of human effort must be invested in shaping a just relationship among states and within states. We must build the peace and keep the peace if we are to be true to the Gospel of Christ and the moral tradition of his Church.

C. The U.S. Bishops and the Nuclear Dilemma

17.   As bishops in the United States, we are teachers in our time of the universal teaching of the Church on war and peace. As citizens of the United States we experience in concrete fashion the responsibility and the apprehension of living in a nuclear nation. Both of these legacies were at the root of our decision in 1980 to prepare the pastoral letter, *The Challenge of Peace.*

18. In *The Challenge of Peace* we asserted that "as a people, we must refuse to legitimate the idea of nuclear war" (no. 131). And we also pointed out that to do this would require of us "not only new ideas and new vision, but what the gospel calls conversion of the heart" (no. 131). Clearly it was as pastoral leaders and moral guides that we entered into the public policy debate on war and peace, and more specifically on nuclear weapons and strategies for their use.

19.   In publishing this report on the fifth anniversary of our 1983 pastoral letter, we once more join the public policy debate from our particular religious and moral perspective. We do not lay claim to any special grasp of military or political realities beyond that of any carefully informed citizens. But we do bring to the debate a special awareness of spiritual/religious realities that we are convinced must help to guide us as a

people concerned to act in a morally acceptable way. We invite all who read this report to do it in the spirit in which we wrote it, the spirit of the psalmist who prayed:

I will hear what God proclaims;
the Lord--for he proclaims peace.
To his people, and to his faithful ones,
and to those who put in him their hope.
(Psalm 85:9)

20. As we issue this report, we assert again that we are teachers, not technicians. We cannot avoid our responsibility to lift up the moral dimensions of the choices before our world and nation. But even as we point out these hard choices, we are filled with a spirit of hope that learning God's ways and walking in his path will bring us to peace. We claim as our own

. . . what Isaiah, son of Amoz, saw concerning
Judah and Jerusalem.
In days to come,
The mountain of the Lord's house
shall be established as the highest mountain
and raised above the hills.
All nations shall stream toward it;
many peoples shall come and say:
"Come, let us climb the Lord's mountain,
to the house of the God of Jacob,
That he may instruct us in his ways,
and we may walk in his paths."
For from Zion shall go forth instruction,
and the word of the Lord from Jerusalem.
He shall judge between nations,
and impose terms on many peoples.
They shall beat their swords into plowshares
and their spears into pruning hooks;

One nation shall not raise the sword against
another,
   nor shall they train for war again.
O house of Jacob, come,
   let us walk in the light of the Lord!
   (Isaiah 2:1-5)

21.   In *The Challenge of Peace* and now in this
report we write as pastors and teachers. We are
convinced that ideas matter, that the way we
understand and think about policies and personal
choices is, in the end, a more potent force than the
material elements of power and technology which
are the external elements of the nuclear
competition. We are equally convinced that values
matter, that both knowledge and power require
direction, guidance, inspiration and restraint.

22.   The contribution of a religious-moral vision to
the nuclear age is precisely to offer a method of
evaluating the choices posed by politics, war and
peace in our time. The reception given *The Challenge of Peace* and the continuing dangers and
possibilities of nuclear politics move us to address
the moral issues once again.

23.   *The Challenge of Peace* concluded its
assessment of nuclear deterrence policy with the
following judgment:

> These considerations of concrete elements of
> nuclear deterrence policy, made in light of
> John Paul II's evaluation, but applying it
> through our own prudential judgments, lead
> us to a strictly conditioned moral
> acceptance of nuclear deterrence. We cannot
> consider it adequate as a long-term basis for
> peace (no. 186).

24. The logic of a "strictly conditioned moral acceptance" of deterrence requires that the "conditions" be examined to see if the policy decisions and programs undertaken in the name of deterrence should be supported, modified or rejected. The pastoral letter recognized this responsibility for a continuing evaluation of the nuclear question. After setting forth the criteria and policy judgments which constitute "the conditions" of the pastoral, the bishops state:

> Clearly, these criteria demonstrate that we cannot approve of every weapons system, strategic doctrine, or policy initiative advanced in the name of strengthening deterrence. On the contrary, these criteria require continual public scrutiny of what our government proposes to do with the deterrent (no. 187).

25. In the normal policy and legislative work of our episcopal conference, as well as in the teaching we do in our dioceses, we have tried as bishops to carry on this task of public scrutiny of deterrence policy. While these daily tasks of education and advocacy are indispensable, the urgency, complexity and changing character of the nuclear challenge require periodic efforts to assess the problem more comprehensively and to sharpen the sense of moral responsibility which nations possessing nuclear arsenals must accept.

D. The Significance of the Present Moment

26. The moral responsibility remains constant, but the conditions in which it is fulfilled change. When *The Challenge of Peace* was written in the early 1980s, there was virtually no serious discussion between the superpowers, there were no prospects for serious arms control and the defense expenditures of both the Soviet Union and the United States were rising sharply. To some degree the situation of the late 1980s must be defined in light of these earlier developments. But there are other characteristics of our present situation which may be more important in the long-run. The December 1987 and May 1988 summit meetings between President Reagan and General Secretary Gorbachev, following upon the Geneva (1985) and Reykjavik (1986) summits, signal a systematic approach to nuclear diplomacy which was barely evident in 1983. The words and deeds of the 1988 summit and subsequent events have raised cautious hopes among the most seasoned observers of superpower relations that an authentically new opportunity for redefining the political relationship of the world's two major military powers may be at hand.

27. The precise definition of the new situation is that it is an opportunity not yet a certainty. For both superpowers, there are internal reasons and international pressures which demand an effort to restructure their political and military competition. For different reasons, the United States and the Soviet Union find the pressure of military spending a debilitating drain on their domestic economic and social progress. Both face sustained international criticism for failures to

place restraints on their strategic competition. To use the words of Pope John Paul II's recent address on the nuclear arms race: "The stockpiling of these weapons in itself constitutes a threat to peace, as well as a provocation to the peoples that lack the essentials for survival and development."[4] In both countries strategic experts recognize that the development of new technologies in the arms race raises the specter of a more dangerous nuclear relationship.

28. The new opportunity which many sense at hand requires a more responsible arms control policy, but it goes beyond a fixation on weapons systems and warhead tabulations. Whether the opportunity to address the deeper political dynamics of the superpower competition can be grasped depends upon the vision, skill, tactics and judgment of two governments. But it also involves the general public in both societies. Our political systems differ radically; the very notion of public opinion is difficult to apply to the two nations. But our publics share a certain tragic destiny: we are both targets; the possibility of a future for our children is always an open question because the weapons that threaten both nations are "absolute weapons." The expression of public opinion bears little similarity because of our differing political systems. But it is not naive to presume that in the face of the common danger of nuclear war the citizens of the United States and the Soviet Union share the same fears and sustain the same hopes. Publics can hope but governments must act. The new dialogue between the superpowers and the first

---

[4] John Paul II, "Address to Diplomatic Corps" (Rome, January 9, 1988), *L'Osservatore Romano,* English weekly edition (January 25, 1988): no. 3, p. 6.

steps taken in 1987 and 1988 to renew the arms control process are the beginning of responsible statesmanship. To grasp the new opportunity will require building carefully but persistently on the foundation of the recent summits.

29. This report is written in response to the charge of Bishop Malone and in light of the changed political climate for arms control. The report is divided into three sections: (1) a review of the moral teaching of *The Challenge of Peace*, (2) an assessment of certain policy developments related to the teaching of the pastoral letter, and (3) a judgment on the moral status of deterrence in 1988.

I. *The Challenge of Peace*
A Summary Statement

30. The distinctive characteristic of *The Challenge of Peace* is that it is a religious-moral evaluation of the political, strategic and technological dimensions of the nuclear age. While the letter is pervaded by a stream of empirical facts and technical distinctions, the reason for the pastoral letter was to submit these data to moral judgment.

31. The moral tradition of the letter is the Catholic ethic on the use or nonuse of force, a tradition which runs from the Sermon on the Mount through the statements of Pope John Paul II. In the pastoral letter, particular weight is given to the papal teaching from Pope Pius XII to Pope John Paul II. It is in recent papal teaching and in the document *Gaudium et Spes (Pastoral Constitution*

on the Church in the Modern World) of Vatican II that the classical tradition of legitimating and limiting the use of force confronts the reality of the nuclear revolution. This confrontation was dramatically symbolized in John Paul II's statement at Hiroshima in 1981: "In the past it was possible to destroy a village, a town, a region, even a country. Now it is the whole planet that has come under threat."[5] This assessment, specifying the qualitatively new destructive potential introduced by nuclear weapons, served as a premise of the more detailed analysis of the pastoral letter.

32. Starting from this premise *The Challenge of Peace* both echoes the papal and conciliar teaching and also expands beyond it, using the resources of biblical and theological scholarship. The pastoral letter contains a series of prudential judgments encompassing both the application of moral principles and the assessment of empirical data. A fundamental teaching characteristic of the pastoral letter is the distinction it repeatedly makes between its affirmation of *moral principles* drawn from the philosophical and theological tradition of the Church and its *specific judgments* of policy and practice:

> In this pastoral letter . . . we address many concrete questions concerning the arms race, contemporary warfare, weapons systems, and negotiating strategies. We do not intend that our treatment of each of these issues carry the same moral authority as

[5] John Paul II, "Address to Scientists and Scholars," no. 4, p. 621.

our statement of universal moral principles and formal church teaching (no. 9).

33. The pastoral letter refuses either to remain at the level of principle or to disguise the fact that moral conclusions about social policy are inevitably dependent on contingent data. It is precisely in the policy section of the pastoral letter that it engages specific issues not addressed in the papal and conciliar teaching. The policy section had three components: moral evaluation of the *use* of nuclear weapons, the strategy of *deterrence* and then a set of policy *prescriptions*.

A. Use of Nuclear Weapons

34. *The Challenge of Peace* made three distinct judgments on the use of nuclear weapons. The judgments comprise a spectrum, moving from absolute prohibition through a prudential proscription to a presumption against use.

35. The absolute prohibition is the pastoral letter's categorical rejection of countercity or countercivilian bombing of any kind: "Under no circumstances may nuclear weapons or other instruments of mass slaughter be used for the purpose of destroying population centers or other predominantly civilian targets" (no. 147).

36. The reaffirmation of one of the core principles of the just-war ethic is specified in the pastoral letter in two ways. First, the principle holds even if our cities have been struck by an adversary. Second, the bishops apply the principle to individual cases in the chain of command: "No Christian can rightfully carry out orders or policies

deliberately aimed at killing noncombatants" (no. 148).

37. A different kind of moral judgment is rendered on the initiation of nuclear war. The absolute categorical character of the first case is replaced by a complex form of reasoning blending moral principles with empirical assessments of the chances of escalation, the possibilities of limiting the effects of using nuclear weapons and the degree of risk involved in taking the world into the nuclear arena. The conclusion of this process of evaluation is the judgment that: "We do not perceive any situation in which the deliberate initiation of nuclear warfare, on however restricted a scale, can be morally justified" (no. 150). This "no first use" conclusion is joined with a broader theme of the pastoral: " . . . [W]e seek to reinforce the barrier against any use of nuclear weapons" (no. 153). The nature of this conclusion against *first use,* contingent as it is on a series of empirical judgments, demands further moral examination in the Church and in the wider society.

38. The third case of use, retaliatory (or second) use in a "limited exchange," typically refers to the kind of nuclear war-fighting envisioned in Central Europe. Here the pastoral letter is less categorical than its opposition to civilian bombing and it is less clear than its opposition to first use. The basic argument of this section is to establish a presumption against second use by raising a series of questions about the possibility of limiting the effects of nuclear weapons. The presumption is not a prohibition; the effect of the presumption, however, is to place the burden of proof on those who assert that "limited use" is politically and morally possible. The logic of the letter is to make the burden of proof a very heavy one. Essentially,

the "just-war" or "limited war" ethic asserts that one should have moral certainty that weapons to be used can be employed within the limits of the twin moral principles of discrimination and proportionality.

39. The questions raised about the possibilities of maintaining a "limited use" of nuclear weapons highlight the multiple pressures which make limitation very unlikely. The dynamic of technological warfare, the normal range of human error, the lack of experience with nuclear war-fighting which all powers fortunately share, all create a tone of radical skepticism in *The Challenge of Peace* about the language of limited war as applied to nuclear conflict. To repeat the judgment of the pastoral letter:

> In the face of this frightening and highly speculative debate on a matter involving millions of human lives, we believe the most effective contribution or moral judgment is to introduce perspectives by which we can assess the empirical debate. Moral perspective should be sensitive not only to the quantitative dimensions of a question but to its psychological, human, and religious characteristics as well. The issue of limited war is not simply the size of weapons contemplated or the strategies projected. The debate should include the psychological and political significance of crossing the boundary from the conventional to the nuclear arena in any form. To cross this divide is to enter a world where we have no experience of control, much testimony against its possibility, and therefore no moral justification for submitting the human community to this

risk.[6] We therefore express our view that the first imperative is to prevent any use of nuclear weapons and our hope that leaders will resist the notion that nuclear conflict can be limited, contained, or won in any traditional sense (no. 161).

40.   Nonetheless, at the conclusion of its assessment of nuclear use, *The Challenge of Peace* has neither advocated any form of use nor has it condemned every conceivable use of nuclear weapons *a priori*. There is in the letter a narrow margin where use has been considered, not condemned but hardly commended. From this narrow margin the pastoral moves to an evaluation of deterrence.

---

[6] "Undoubtedly aware of the long and detailed technical debate on limited war, Pope John Paul II highlighted the unacceptable moral risk of crossing the threshold to nuclear war in his "Angelus Message" of December 13, 1981: 'I have, in fact, the deep conviction that, in the light of a nuclear war's effects, which can be scientifically foreseen as certain, the only choice that is morally and humanly valid is represented by the reduction of nuclear armaments, while waiting for their future complete elimination, carried out simultaneously by all the parties, by means of explicit agreements and with the commitment of accepting effective controls.' *The Challenge of Peace*, footnote 70, quoting *Peace and Disarmament: Documents of the World Council of Churches and the Roman Catholic Church* (Geneva and Rome: World Council of Churches and Vatican, 1982), p. 240."

B. The Strategy of Deterrence

41. *The Challenge of Peace* based its evaluation of deterrence on the just-war ethic, guided by *Gaudium et Spes* (1965) and by Pope John Paul II's *Message to the United Nations* (1982). The conciliar text had described the moral dilemma of deterrence, but had not entered into a detailed moral judgment. Pope John Paul II had gone beyond the Council: "In current conditions 'deterrence' based on balance, certainly not as an end in itself but as a step on the way toward a progressive disarmament, may still be judged morally acceptable."[7] *The Challenge of Peace* went beyond the papal judgment to probe the logic of conditional approval and to specify the meaning of "conditional." The letter examined theories of deterrence, the arguments about nuclear "war-fighting" as a strategy and the debate which has surrounded plans for nuclear targeting. Without repeating the full argument here we call attention to the detailed assessment of these questions found in paragraphs 178-185 of *The Challenge of Peace.*

42. The "dilemma of deterrence" cited above is the problem of how to sustain a credible deterrent (to prevent nuclear attack while refraining from any intent to target civilians or to violate the limits of proportionality). Anyone who has tried theoretically or practically to reconcile these objectives knows the inherent tension between them. In *The Challenge of Peace* we acknowledged the need for a deterrence strategy but also asserted

---

[7] John Paul II, "Message to U.N. Special Session on Disarmament 1982," no. 8, cited in *The Challenge of Peace*, no. 173.

that "not all forms of deterrence are morally acceptable" (no. 178).

43. The principal limit defining a justifiable deterrent is the prohibition against directly targeting or striking civilians. The pastoral letter asserts the prohibition, which we reaffirm here, and summarizes an exchange of the NCCB and the U.S. Government about the U.S. position on targeting doctrine.[8]

44. The second limit placed on justifiable deterrence is the principle of proportionality. It is particularly needed to address two questions analyzed in the pastoral letter. The first is the damage done by attacks on "military or industrial" targets located near civilian centers. Second is the damage envisioned in various forms of nuclear warfighting strategies.

45. The first problem is inherent in the existing deterrence strategies of both superpowers, since each targets the industrial capacity of the other. There will inevitably be continuing arguments about what constitutes a "proportionate threat" to deter or what is "proportionate damage," but we remain convinced that

> . . . there are actions which can be decisively judged to be disproportionate. A narrow adherence exclusively to the principle of noncombatant immunity as a criterion for policy is an inadequate moral posture, for it ignores some evil and unacceptable consequences. Hence, we cannot be satisfied that the assertion of an intention not to strike civilians directly, or even the most honest effort to implement

---

[8] See *The Challenge of Peace*, no. 179, footnote 81.

that intention, by itself constitutes a "moral policy" for the use of nuclear weapons (no. 181).

46. The second problem, war-fighting strategies, arises from the quest for a coherent connection between "deterrence and use" policies and from the search for "discriminate deterrence." While acknowledging the concerns which drive both of these endeavors and welcoming any effort to guarantee the immunity of the civilian population, we remain convinced that such proposals should not be understood as an assurance that nuclear war is subject to precise or rational limits. The "dilemma of deterrence" is not ameliorated by notions that nuclear weapons are "normal," "controlled" instruments of military policy. The logic of the pastoral letter, reasserted here, is to build a barrier against nuclear use and to confine the role of deterrence to "the specific objective of preventing the use of nuclear weapons . . . ."(no. 185)[9]

47. The conclusion of *The Challenge of Peace* on deterrence was cited earlier in this report, but it deserves repetition here:

> These considerations of concrete elements of nuclear deterrence policy, made in light of John Paul II's evaluation, but applying it through our own prudential judgments, lead us to a strictly conditioned moral acceptance of nuclear deterrence. We cannot consider it adequate as a long-term basis for peace (no. 186).

48. The "strict conditions" which the pastoral imposed on deterrence involved two kinds of

---

[9] Cf. ibid., nos. 140, 153.

restraints. The first involved a "temporal" dimension; in the language of the pastoral, deterrence is not a "long-term" answer to the nuclear question. The temporal aspect of conditionality was not intended to place a moral straightjacket on policy. It did not, for example, set an exact timetable after which the moral acceptance would be exhausted. This is too simple an instrument of assessment for the deterrence relationship which is dynamic in character and dependent upon the choices of other actors besides the United States. Such a mechanistic view also fails to consider that the policy of deterrence is comprised by several elements, some of which can be acceptable while others stand in need of criticism and change.

49. The "temporal condition" contained in *The Challenge of Peace* is an attempt to reflect and specify the meaning of the papal dictum that deterrence should be seen as part of a complex process leading to a new political relationship. In this sense the temporal condition is meant to test "the direction" of the deterrence relationship and the policies which sustain it. Are these policies moving toward progressive disarmament? In the short term, are these policies moving in the direction of reducing the likelihood of nuclear use, enhancing the stability of the superpower relationship and making possible quantitative and qualitative reductions in the arms race?

50. The second condition placed on deterrence policy by the pastoral letter is designed to test the "character" or the "component elements" of the deterrent. The test applied is rooted in moral categories, using the principles of proportionality, noncombatant immunity, last resort and the risks implied in different forms of deterrence policy.

Testing the character of weapons, forms of deployment and declaratory policy in this way corresponds to the classical concerns of arms control, which stress less the numbers of weapons in the deterrence relationship than the impact certain weapons have on the stability of the nuclear balance.

51.   The intent to test both the "direction" of deterrence policy and the "character" of specific weapons in the deterrent led *The Challenge of Peace* to set forth specific criteria and conditions for moral judgment about deterrence.

C. Criteria and Conditions for Policy Evaluation

52.   These criteria and conditions should be used together as a framework for assessing several aspects of nuclear strategy.

Criteria for Conditional Acceptance of Deterrence:

(1) If nuclear deterrence exists only to prevent the *use* of nuclear weapons by others, then proposals to go beyond this to planning for prolonged periods of repeated nuclear strikes and counterstrikes, or "prevailing" in nuclear war, are not acceptable. They encourage notions that nuclear war can be engaged in with tolerable human and moral consequences. Rather, we must continually say "no" to the idea of nuclear war.

(2) If nuclear deterrence is our goal, "sufficiency" to deter is an adequate

strategy; the quest for nuclear superiority must be rejected.

(3) Nuclear deterrence should be used as a step on the way toward progressive disarmament. Each proposed addition to our strategic system or change in strategic doctrine must be assessed precisely in light of whether it will render steps toward "progressive disarmament" more or less likely (no. 188).

Conditions for Conditional Acceptance of Deterrence:

In light of the criteria we opposed the following proposals:

(1) The addition of weapons which are likely to be vulnerable to attack, yet also possess a "prompt hard-target kill" capability that threatens to make the other side's retaliatory forces vulnerable. Such weapons may seem to be useful primarily in a first strike; we resist such weapons for this reason and we oppose Soviet deployment of such weapons which generate fear of a first strike against U.S. forces.

(2) The willingness to foster strategic planning which seeks a nuclear war-fighting capability that goes beyond the limited function of deterrence outlined in this letter.

(3) Proposals which have the effect of lowering the nuclear threshold and blurring the difference between nuclear and conventional weapons (no. 190).

In support of the concept of "sufficiency" as an adequate deterrent, and in light of the existing size and composition of both the U.S. and Soviet strategic arsenals, we recommended:

(1) Support for immediate, bilateral, verifiable agreements to halt the testing, production and deployment of new nuclear weapons systems.
(2) Support for negotiated bilateral deep cuts in the arsenals of both superpowers, particularly those weapons systems which have destabilizing characteristics. . . .
(3) Support for early and successful conclusion of negotiations of a comprehensive test ban treaty.
(4) Removal by all parties of short-range nuclear weapons which multiply dangers disproportionate to their deterrent value.
(5) Removal by all parties of nuclear weapons from areas where they are likely to be overrun in the early stages of war, thus forcing rapid and uncontrollable decisions on their use.
(6) Strengthening of command and control over nuclear weapons to prevent inadvertent and unauthorized use (no. 191).

53. In congressional testimony of 1984, Cardinal Bernardin and Cardinal O'Connor returned to the theme of setting forth additional criteria by which proposed changes in the deterrent arsenal should be judged. Against the background of debates concerning the wisdom of deploying the MX missile or proceeding toward defensive systems, they offered the following guideline:

If a particular system is found to be of dubious strategic value (i.e., not absolutely necessary to preserve our deterrence posture) and yet is certain to cost large sums of money, then these two criteria lead us to recommend against the system in question.[10]

54. The application and refinement of these criteria and conditions to a range of policy questions is the task of the rest of this report. As we begin the process of evaluating policy choices and technological trends, we reaffirm a key guideline for interpreting our position as bishops on these complex questions. The guideline is found in *The Challenge of Peace*, but applies with equal force to this report:

> In this pastoral letter, . . . we address many concrete questions concerning the arms race, contemporary warfare, weapons systems, and negotiating strategies. We do not intend that our treatment of each of these issues carry the same moral authority as our statement of universal moral principles and formal church teaching. . . . When making applications of these principles we realize--and we wish readers to recognize-- that prudential judgments are involved based on specific circumstances which can change or which can be interpreted

---

[10] Cardinal Bernardin and Archbishop O'Connor, Testimony for the U.S. Catholic Conference on U.S. Arms Control Policy before the Committee on Foreign Affairs, U.S. House of Representative (June 26, 1984), p. 150, *Origins* 14:10 (August 9, 1984): p. 157.

differently by people of good will . . . (nos. 9-10).

II. Policy Developments Assessment and Recommendations

55. Three areas of nuclear policy are directly relevant to the conditions set by *The Challenge of Peace:* (1) the politics and strategy of arms control policy, (2) technological developments and the arms race, and (3) the economic impact of defense spending.

A. Arms Control Policy

56. Arms control is fundamentally a political process which Catholic teaching sees as a step toward disarmament. Arms control should be viewed, therefore, in light of the political relationship which has prevailed between the superpowers and the new opportunity, noted above, which presents fundamental choices to the Soviet Union and the United States.

57. The new opportunity, even if utilized, should not be expected to dissipate or dissolve the basic realities of U.S.-Soviet relations. As *The Challenge of Peace* observed, the two nations are divided by history, philosophy, polity and conflicting interests. The possibility which may be open is not to transcend these fundamental differences, but to regulate the competitive relationship with new criteria. The superpowers

confront each other directly, through their European allies, and in a variety of ways in the Southern Hemisphere.

58. The capabilities of both nuclear giants to create a nuclear crisis or a nuclear catastrophe for the rest of the world is the most threatening way in which their relationship affects others. But beyond the nuclear question, the political role of the Soviet Union and the United States remains decisive for the safety, stability and welfare of the international community. In the European theater one effect of the Intermediate-Range Nuclear Forces (INF) Treaty is to increase the significance of the political questions both within the alliances and between the superpowers directly. The most intractable issues between the superpowers for much of the last 15 years have been their involvement in regional conflicts from the Horn of Africa to Afghanistan and the Persian Gulf to Nicaragua and Central America. This report focuses upon the specifically nuclear relationship, but it would be a narrow view of the challenge of the present moment if the wider political context of the superpower relationship were ignored. Arms control can be a catalyst to an improved political relationship, and changes in the political context of superpower relations can open the road to new steps in controlling weaponry. This reciprocal relationship of politics and strategy means, in part, that a failure to move forward on the arms control front will very likely make progress in other areas of U.S.-Soviet relations more difficult.

59. Essentially the task of testing the new opportunity in superpower relations will require both political vision and strategic wisdom. The latter is needed to restrain the nuclear competition and to reduce its component elements. The former is

required to set limits on the political competition which will be in the interests of the major powers, but will also decrease the hold of bipolar politics on others in the international community.

60. Turning specifically to arms control, both Pope John Paul II's statements linking acceptance of deterrence with movement toward disarmament and the pastoral letter's endorsement of a series of arms control measures give this topic a central place in evaluating events since 1983. The following developments stand out.

1. The INF Treaty

61. The INF Treaty, signed by Mr. Reagan and Mr. Gorbachev on December 8, 1987, represents the first bilateral arms control accomplishment since the SALT I Treaty (1972). The treaty provides for abolition of two classes of nuclear delivery systems (intermediate-range and shorter-range missiles). Although these weapons constitute a small percentage of the strategic arsenals of the super-powers, the dual significance of reconstituting the arms control process with a treaty and of achieving actual reductions in nuclear weaponry constitute steps in accord with the criteria of *The Challenge of Peace*, and we have supported ratification of the treaty in congressional testimony.

The INF Treaty, in the view of its supporters and its critics, inevitably points beyond itself to other larger arms control questions. It was also depicted in this light in the statement of Pope John Paul II who devoted much of his annual *Address to the Diplomatic Corps* to the INF Treaty and to the issue of nuclear disarmament:

> Nuclear disengagement, which for the time being still involves only a very limited

proportion of the respective arsenals, may now be pursued without the global military balance being called into question, to the point of reaching the lowest level compatible with mutual security . . . . According to the protagonists, the agreement on intermediate nuclear weapons is more a point of departure than an end in itself. It was the occasion for the two signatories to affirm their determination to accelerate the negotiations taking place on ballistic nuclear weapons, which are the most menacing of all. It is important not only to mitigate but to remove definitively the threat of a nuclear catastrophe. It is certainly the wish of the entire international community that such talks succeed as soon as possible, inspired by the same principles.[11]

2. The Nuclear and Space Talks (NST)

62.   The negotiations on strategic forces and space-based defenses are the next step beyond the INF Treaty. In line with the criteria of *The Challenge of Peace*, we support the "deep cuts" formula (1600 launchers and 6000 warheads) which is being used in these negotiations. We welcome these proposed reductions even while noting the accepted fact that the *kinds* of weapons which are constrained or reduced are the more important criterion than the *number* reduced. In the NST, there are important quantitative (number) and

---

[11] John Paul II, "Address to Diplomatic Corps," nos. 3, 4, p. 7.

qualitative (kind) reductions which are being negotiated. These negotiations deserve and have our strong support.

3. Existing Treaties

63.   While NST proceed, we find it imprudent and counterproductive to erode or dismantle fragile restraints on an arms competition vigorously in progress. Hence, we support maintaining the limits established in the SALT I-ABM Treaty on defensive systems, and we oppose the U.S. decision not to abide by the SALT II limits on offensive forces. Finally, we reaffirm the recommendation of the 1983 pastoral that negotiation should be vigorously pursued on a comprehensive test ban treaty.

4. New Deployments

64.   The INF Treaty and the NST must be seen within the context of other developments in the 1980s. Even as the superpowers have carried on nuclear negotiations, they have also proceeded with nuclear modernization programs (i.e., the development of new weapons) which are the product of decisions taken in the 1970s and early 1980s. Since the 1970s, the Soviet Union has deployed four new strategic systems and several thousand warheads. The United States is carrying forward new deployments on every leg of the strategic triad (land-based missiles--ICBMs, submarine-launched missiles--SLBMs and bombers). Both the Soviet Union and the United States, therefore, are deploying weapons which, in both number and kind, run contrary to the conditions of *The Challenge of Peace*. The pastoral letter

specifically cited weapons which increase the incentive "to preempt" (strike first) in a crisis as particularly undesirable. The Soviet Union's deployment of the SS-18s and its plan to deploy SS-24s, along with the U.S. deployment of the MX run directly counter to this recommendation. The U.S. planned deployment of the D-5 submarine-launched missile (Trident II) involves a more complex judgment; its range and relative invulnerability can add stability in a crisis, but its accuracy and yield run counter to the criteria of the· pastoral letter.

5. Independent Initiatives

65. During the 1980s both the United States and the Soviet Union have taken steps which fit the category of "independent initiatives" found in *The Challenge of Peace,* but in each case the initiative was not reciprocated. The NATO alliance made decisions in 1980 and again in 1983 to withdraw a total of 2400 battlefield nuclear weapons from the European theater. In August 1985 the Soviet Union announced a unilateral moratorium on nuclear testing which it extended through 1986; the Soviets have now resumed nuclear testing.

6. Conventional Arms Control

66. This assessment of certain major trends in superpower relations does not capture all the pertinent dimensions of the arms control picture. Two major areas which will have an increasing importance in the 1990s are conventional arms control and non-proliferation policies. The legitimate concern paid to the unique qualities of the nuclear danger should not distract needed

attention from the control of conventional armaments. This is a global problem, going far beyond the bounds of direct superpower relations and beyond the interaction of NATO and the Warsaw Pact. The more than 150 conflicts since World War II have all used conventional weapons, many of them supplied by the industrialized nations to parties in the developing world. The "North-South" dimension of conventional arms trade and the need for regional restraints in the arms competition would require a separate report. In the encyclical *On Social Concern,*[12] Pope John Paul II identified the conventional arms trade as one of the principal ways in which the East-West superpower competition distorts and corrupts the quest for authentic development in the Third World:

> If arms production is a serious disorder in the present world with regard to true human needs and the employment of the means capable of satisfying those needs, *the arms trade* is equally to blame. Indeed, with reference to the latter it must be added that the *moral judgment is even more severe.* As we all know, this is a trade without frontiers, capable of crossing even the barriers of the blocs. It knows how to overcome the division between East and West, and above all the one between North and South, to the point--and this is more serious--of pushing its way into the *different sections* which make up the

---

[12] John Paul II, *On Social Concern (Sollicitudo Rei Socialis)* (Washington, D.C.: USCC Office of Publishing and Promotion Services, 1988).

southern hemisphere. We are thus confronted with a strange phenomenon: while economic aid and development plans meet with the obstacle of insuperable ideological barriers and with tariff and trade barriers, *arms* of whatever origin circulate with almost total freedom all over the world. And as the recent document of the Pontifical Commission "Justitia et Pax" on the international debt points out, everyone knows that in certain cases the capital lent by the developed world has been used in the underdeveloped world to buy weapons (no. 24).

67. In the East-West framework the relationship between nuclear and conventional arms control will be increasingly important. Precisely if it is possible to proceed with "deep cuts" of 30-50 percent in strategic arsenals will the need to evaluate a corresponding move on the conventional front become clear. In *The Challenge of Peace* we said that our emphasis on controlling the nuclear arms race was not intended to make the world safe for conventional war. To address this concern, the future of arms control negotiations will have to pay greater attention to relating progress on the nuclear front to steps on conventional arms control. In his assessment of the INF Treaty, Pope John Paul II made two points relevant to conventional arms control. First, the objective of negotiations should aim at ensuring security at the lowest possible level of conventional arms which is compatible with "reasonable requirements for defense."[13]

---

[13] John Paul II, "Address to Diplomatic Corps," no. 4, p. 7.

Second, even granting the first criterion, the pope still warned that "there is need to avoid at all cost a new form of escalation in conventional weapons which would be hazardous and ruinous."[14]

68. If both stable deterrence is to be maintained and a new round of conventional escalation to be avoided, the proposed new negotiations for NATO and the Warsaw Pact on conventional arms will have to be pursued with a clearer policy focus and much greater political urgency than has marked much of the now moribund negotiations on Mutual Balanced Force Reductions. In the West particularly these conventional negotiations will require particular attention to the political dimensions of the alliance relationship.

7. Nuclear Non-proliferation

69. The second neglected area of the 1980s has been the problem of nuclear proliferation. Since the Non-Proliferation Treaty (NPT) came into force (1970), a framework for controlling the proliferation of nuclear weapons has existed. The non-proliferation negotiations and the non-proliferation order established by the treaty essentially constituted a compact between the major nuclear states and the nonnuclear powers. Essential to the compact was the commitment of the superpowers to restrain and reverse the "vertical" arms race in return for a pledge from nonnuclear states to refrain from "horizontal" proliferation.

70. In 1995 the NPT is due for renewal; it is clear that several key nonnuclear states are dissatisfied with the present regime and the role of the nuclear

---

[14] Ibid.

powers in it. This is not the only, or perhaps not even the principal threat to non-proliferation. Local and regional problems may in the final analysis be the decisive determinant in a proliferation decision. But the status of the compact on vertical and horizontal proliferation is directly under the control of the Soviet Union and the United States. The imperative to renew progress on arms control before the NPT is due for renewal is a primary consideration in the arms control picture.

71. Finally, the assessment of specific aspects of U.S.-Soviet policies on arms control does not adequately convey the critical character of the present moment. In *The Challenge of Peace* we noted that one of the distinguishing elements of the nuclear age is that we cannot afford one serious mistake. The consequences would be catastrophic--probably beyond our capacity to imagine. In the United States we have known the fear generated by Three Mile Island and the Soviet and European populations have experienced the reality of Chernobyl, but these events are mere shadows compared to the devastation and terror which even a "limited" nuclear exchange would produce.

72. The nuclear debate of the 1980s has resulted in a higher level of public sensitivity to the fragile hold we have on our common nuclear future and an increased awareness of the moral dangers of the nuclear age. Even those in the expert community who stress that deterrence is "robust" or "stable" acknowledge that we cannot simply presume that deterrence which "has worked" for 40 years will surely continue "to work." The possibilities of technical accident, human miscalculation or diplomatic crisis--taken singly or together--pose

permanent threats to the system which the superpowers now rely upon for "security."

73. These possibilities of failure exist in the very nature of nuclear deterrence. The more troubling fact is that recent trends in the character of weapons being deployed accentuate the dangers of deterrence. Large, MIRVed, very accurate missiles, often deployed as vulnerable targets, tilt the nuclear balance toward a preemptive posture on both sides. In the technical literature on the nuclear balance, analysts of quite different policy persuasions agree that present trends are not conducive to deterrence stability. From this analysis the question arises whether it is possible and useful to conceive of "going beyond deterrence." *The Challenge of Peace* asserted that deterrence is not a long-term solution to a sound security system. Recently Pope John Paul returned to this theme himself:

> Such a strategy, applied in a context of detente and cooperation, must lead to a progressive search for a new balance at the lowest possible level of weapons, so as to arrive eventually at the elimination of the atomic weapon itself. In this matter one must move towards total disarmament. May the protagonists understand that their mutual security is always furthered by an interpenetration of interests and vital relations![15]

74. All commentators, whether they are political analysts, strategists or moralists, find it easier to propose going beyond deterrence than to prescribe the steps for accomplishing this task. One

---

[15] Ibid., no. 5, p. 7.

direction involves trying to realize some of the potential in the U.S.-Soviet political relationship described above. As long as nuclear weapons exist, deterrence will be an inherent fact of the superpower relationship. But improvement in the political atmosphere can, over time, reduce the significance of nuclear deterrence in the total relationship.

75.   This political approach will have to be joined with a strategy of arms control. The objectives of arms control are more modest than disarmament, but the latter is impossible without the former. Moreover, arms control which is not yet disarmament still can contribute to a safer world by stressing the objectives of survivable forces with clearly verifiable limits. Arms control can channel the superpower competition in the interim while other, more profound efforts seek to transform the political relationship. The fundamental importance of arms control needs to be reaffirmed in this evaluation. It is one way we take hold of our common nuclear future with the Soviet Union.

76.   In light of this assessment, our evaluation of the last five years does not produce a single simple conclusion. The INF Treaty has been signed and some other possibilities are now on the negotiating table which, if completed, would fulfill some key criteria of the pastoral letter. But in the face of this still uncertain promise, there stands the historical fact of major additions to the strategic arsenals of both superpowers, weapons whose character and numbers decidedly increase the danger of nuclear war occurring. This pattern of policy is not adequate to the moral danger of the age that these arsenals, by miscalculation or mistake, will escape human control and destroy in

an hour what humanity has taken centuries to build and shape.

77. The "conditional acceptance" of deterrence found in *The Challenge of Peace* is directly tied to the pursuit of arms control and, ultimately, disarmament. The arms control successes cited in this report should be welcomed. But the opportunities missed when arms control was shunted aside for years at a time deserve equal attention. To some degree the arms control successes of the present are compensating for lost opportunities in the past decade. Failure to pursue arms control systematically erodes support for deterrence. In the coming decade the moral legitimacy of deterrence policy will be tested precisely by the linkage of deterrence, arms control and disarmament.

B. Technological Developments

78. Technology acts as a two-edged sword in the nuclear competition; some technological changes (e.g., Permissive Action Links) contribute to increasing control of nuclear weapons; other developments (e.g., MIRVing) have had a long-term destabilizing impact. Since 1983, developments in missile accuracy, anti-satellite weapons and stealth technology have continued the bivalent influence of technology on the arms race. The dilemmas of command, control and communication systems (C3) illustrate this well. Some improvements in C3 are dangerous if they enhance "war-fighting" capabilities and feed the illusion of surviving an extended nuclear exchange. Other improvements would decrease reliance on strategies of launch under attack or launch on warning, and so enhance the stability of deterrence

in crisis. These latter improvements are at present hardly keeping up with the expansion and evolution of weaponry; they require vigorous attention at the level of technology and at the level of superpower political understanding.

79. But the most significant change by far in the area of technology and policy has been the proposal of President Reagan to pursue a defense against ballistic missiles. Technically described as the Strategic Defense Initiative (SDI), it originated on March 23, 1983 in a presidential address to the nation. The key passages of the address are well known:

> Let me share with you a vision of the future which offers hope. It is that we embark on a program to counter the awesome Soviet missile threat with measures that are defensive . . . . What if free people could live secure in the knowledge that their security did not rest upon the threat of instant U.S. retaliation to deter a Soviet attack, that we could intercept and destroy strategic ballistic missiles before they reached our own soil or that of our allies?[16]

80. The proposal, described as "radical" by both then Secretary of Defense Weinberger and critics of the SDI, holds particular importance in any review of *The Challenge of Peace* for three reasons. First, the proposal was made only weeks before publication of the pastoral; so there is no treatment of defensive systems in the letter. Second, the

---

[16] President Reagan, "Launching the SDI," cited in Z. Brzezinski, ed., *Promise or Peril: The Strategic Defense Initiative* (Washington, D.C.: Ethics and Public Policy Center, 1986), pp. 48-49.

defensive proposal now permeates the debate about nuclear policy. A recent report of the Aspen Institute Strategy Group observed: "Virtually all issues related to arms control, alliance security, and Soviet-American strategic relations are now linked to SDI in one way or another."[17] Third, the proponents of SDI, from the president to the secretary of defense to supporters in the public debate, all have made the claim that SDI constitutes a superior moral policy to that of deterrence as we have known it in the nuclear age. Individually and collectively these reasons point toward the need to address the SDI proposal. Here, we seek to outline the character of the SDI debate, using representative public positions, and then to comment on it in light of relevant moral principles.

1. SDI: What Is It?

81. In simple terms, SDI is a research program charged with investigating the technological possibilities of defense against ballistic missiles. But the description cannot remain simple, for even within the Reagan Administration there is a certain pluralism in describing the scope and purpose of SDI. The president's address described the goal of the program in terms of rendering nuclear weapons "impotent and obsolete." Mr. Weinberger described the meaning of the SDI proposal as a "radical rejection of benign acquiescence in reliance upon the threat of mutual

---

[17] Aspen Strategy Group Report, *The Strategic Defense Initiative and American Security* (Lanham, Md., University Press of America, 1987), p. ix.

destruction."[18] Taken at face value these descriptions depict a program designed *to transcend* a policy of deterrence based on the threat of nuclear retaliation.

82.   Almost from the beginning of the SDI program, however, official statements have included a more modest goal, not to transcend deterrence but *to enhance* deterrence. In 1986 Mr. Weinberger spoke of three justifications for the SDI program: to hedge against a Soviet breakthrough on defensive technologies, to guard against a Soviet breakout of the ABM Treaty, and, finally, "the very real possibility that American science and technology will achieve what appears to some to be an impossible dream."[19] The first two reasons do not transcend deterrence, the third looks to that goal.

83.   Enhancing deterrence means using defensive systems in a mode which will complicate Soviet planning for a preemptive strike against American land-based ICBMs. The administration case is neither a pure instance of area defense (of population) nor point defense (of missiles) but a mix of partial area and partial point defense designed

---

[18] C.W. Weinberger, Secretary of Defense, *Annual Report to the Congress Fiscal Year 1987* (Washington, D.C.: U.S. Government Printing Office, 1986), p.73.

[19] C.W. Weinberger, "U.S. Defense Strategy," *Foreign Affairs* 64:4 (1986): p. 682. For the Reagan Administration's evaluation of Soviet activities on defensive systems, see, e.g., *Soviet Strategic Defense Programs* (Washington, D.C.; Department of State and Department of Defense, 1985).

to forestall Soviet confidence in resorting to a nuclear attack.[20]

84.   These two descriptions of the SDI (transcending and enhancing deterrence) have created a certain confusion in the public debate, since the technological challenge and strategic rationale for the two are substantially different. In spite of a less than clear policy focus, the administration has been quite successful in securing congressional support for SDI. A recent congressional staff report records the growth in SDI appropriations:

> In FY 1985 the Administration requested $1.78 billion for SDI, a 79 percent nominal increase over the previous year's funding level. Congress approved $1.40 billion for FY 1985, a 41 percent increase. In FY 1986, the Administration requested $3.72 billion for SDI, a 166 percent increase over FY 1985. Congress approved $2.76 billion, a 97 percent increase. And in FY 1987, the Administration requested $4.8 billion for SDI, a 74 percent increase. Congress approved $3.2 billion, a 16 percent increase.[21]

---

[20] K. Adelman, Director of U.S. Arms Control and Disarmament Agency, Testimony before NCCB Ad Hoc Committee on the Moral Evaluation of Deterrence, March 27, 1987.

[21] *SDI: Progress and Challenges--Part Two: Staff Report Submitted to Senator Proxmire and Senator Johnston* (March 19, 1987), p. 3. (Since the staff report was published, the Congress decided to fund SDI at $3.9 billion for FY 1988.)

85. While these statistics indicate a certain congressional reserve about the program, the significant increases should not be overlooked; spending rose by 41 percent, 97 percent and 16 percent in nominal terms over a three year period. The congressional study specifies the meaning of these expenditures: "The SDI program's budget has more than tripled since its inception, it has become the largest military research program in DOD-- the department's top strategic priority--and its funding level now surpasses the combined technology base funding for the Army, Navy and Air Force."[22]

86. In addition to an aggressive legislative program, the administration has expanded the policy framework in its presentation of the SDI. Two speeches by senior State Department officials set the policy rationale and criteria for SDI. In January 1985, then Under Secretary of State Kenneth Dam set forth the "strategic concept" which the administration is using to link its SDI program with its arms control philosophy:

> For the next 10 years, we should seek a radical reduction in the number and power of existing and planned offensive and defensive nuclear arms, whether landbased, spacebased, or otherwise. We should even now be looking forward to a period of transition, beginning possibly 10 years from now, to effective nonnuclear defensive forces, including defenses against offensive nuclear arms. This period of transition should lead to the eventual elimination of nuclear arms, both offensive and defensive. A nuclear-free world is an

---

[22] Ibid.

ultimate objective to which we, the Soviet Union, and all other nations can agree.[23]

87. In February 1985, Ambassador Paul H. Nitze moved the SDI debate forward by establishing criteria which any deployment would have to satisfy. The Nitze criteria have become a canonical reference in the SDI debate, with both critics and supporters of the proposal appealing to them. Nitze reiterated Dam's argument that the objective of the SDI was "a cooperative effort with the Soviet Union, hopefully leading to an agreed transition toward effective nonnuclear defenses that might make possible the eventual elimination of nuclear weapons."[24] Movement toward this goal involves three stages: the near-term, a transition period and an ultimate phase. In the near-term, deterrence based on nuclear retaliation will continue to structure the nuclear relationship, but research in defensive technologies and arms control aimed at "radical reductions" in offensive forces would both be pushed vigorously.

88. In the transitional period--the key moment-- greater reliance will be placed on defensive systems. The criteria which must be met in any deployment are technological feasibility, survivability and cost-effectiveness.[25] If defensive systems cannot be deployed in a survivable manner, they become tempting targets and increase strategic instability. If these systems are not "cost-effective

---

[23] K.W. Dam, "Geneva and Beyond: New Arms Control Negotiations," *Department of State Bulletin* 85:2096 (March 1985): p. 39.

[24] P.H. Nitze, "On the Road to a More Stable Peace," *Department of State Bulletin* 85:2097 (April 1985): p. 27.

[25] Ibid., p. 28.

at the margin," then it will be cheaper for the adversary to build countermeasures. The transition period would be, in Nitze's words, "tricky"; it would require progress in controlling offensive weapons, and it would have to be executed in cooperation with the Soviets. Provided the conditions of the first two periods are met, the ultimate phase of the new strategic concept could, in Nitze's view, lead to "the reduction of nuclear weapons down to zero."[26]

89.　Both the specific proposal of the SDI--a multilayered defense designed to attack ballistic missiles in the four stages of their trajectory (boost phase, post-boost phase, midcourse flight and terminal phase)--and the strategic concept sustaining it have come under criticism. The public debate has focused on the technological feasibility of SDI and its impact on strategic stability and arms control.

2. SDI: Technology, Strategy and Arms Control

90.　The nuclear debate has always had a forbiddingly technical character, but the SDI controversy has raised the technical discussion to a new plateau of complexity. Both the density of the technological data and the diversity of expert opinions make the debate about the feasibility of the system a crucial point in the policy arena. Diversity of opinion should not be taken to mean the experts are equally divided; there seems to be substantially more doubters in the scientific community than advocates of SDI.

91.　Yet the administration has continued to be optimistic in its assessment of the feasibility of SDI--at least the SDI designed *to enhance*

---

26 Ibid.

deterrence. Paul H. Nitze spoke in March 1986 of "impressive advances" in the investigation of SDI technology. The progress is such that "the United States has good reason to believe that SDI technologies hold the promise for feasible, survivable, and cost-effective defenses."[27] Dr. George Keyworth, science adviser to President Reagan when SDI was proposed, spoke to the NCCB Ad Hoc Committee in terms which seemed to reach beyond Nitze's cautious "promise" to a tangible product. Describing the technological progress made since 1983, Keyworth said:

> That progress meant that by the time of the Geneva Summit in 1985 we could, with some confidence, picture a boost-phase defense system driven by any of several *different* technologies . . . . These numbers describe an awesome defensive capability; a battery of perhaps a dozen such weapons would so overwhelm the offensive forces that countering them by proliferation would be out of the question. So if in March of 1983 we were asking IF we could develop SDI, we can now ask *how* best to choose from those that are emerging.[28]

92. The evaluations of feasibility coming from other voices in the scientific and strategic community have often been notably more cautious. Perhaps the preeminent critical contribution to the technical debate from outside the administration

---

[27] P.H. Nitze, "The Promise of SDI," *Department of State Bulletin* 86:2110 (May 1986): p. 55.

[28] G.A. Keyworth, II, "SDI and Arms Control," Testimony to NCCB Ad Hoc Committee on the Moral Evaluation of Deterrence, December 5, 1986, pp. 12-13.

has been the report commissioned by the American Physical Society (APS). The APS convened a study group "to evaluate the status of the science and technology of directed energy weapons (DEW)."[29] The group was established because of "the divergence of views within the scientific community"[30] on SDI. The 400-page study is devoted exclusively to directed energy weapons (only one possible SDI technology), but its detailed assessment lends weight to its cautious prediction:

> Although substantial progress has been made in many technologies of DEW over the last two decades, the Study Group finds significant gaps in the scientific and engineering understanding of many issues associated with the development of these technologies. Successful resolution of these issues is critical for the extrapolation to performance levels that would be required in an effective ballistic missile defense system. At present, there is insufficient information to decide whether the required extrapolations can or cannot be achieved. Most crucial elements required for a DEW system need improvements of several orders of magnitude. Because the elements are interrelated, the improvements must be achieved in a mutually consistent manner. We estimate that even in the best of

[29] N. Bloembergen (Harvard University), C.K. Patel (AT&T Bell Laboratories), co-chairs, et al. *Report to the American Physical Society of the Study Group on Science and Technology of Directed Energy Weapons,* p. 1. [Published in *Reviews of Modern Physics* 59:3 Part II (July 1987).]
[30] Ibid.

circumstances, a decade or more of intensive research would be required to provide the technical knowledge needed for an informed decision about the potential effectiveness and survivability of directed energy weapon systems. In addition, the important issues of overall system integration and effectiveness depend critically upon information that, to our knowledge, does not yet exist.[31]

93.   The APS Study Group eschewed the policy issues of arms control, strategic stability and cost. Two other recent studies are more policy-oriented, joining their judgments on the feasibility of SDI to arms control concerns. The Aspen Strategy Group Report argues that meeting the administration's own criteria of survivability and cost-effectiveness would effectively rule out any deployment of space-based defenses until well into the 1990s. The strategy group specifies three challenges facing SDI:

1.   many innovations which assist the defense also enhance offensive capabilities;
2.   effective boost-phase defense "seems problematic"; and
3.   terminal phase defense seems unlikely using SDI's nonnuclear technology.

The Aspen Group advocates a SDI research program, but one carried out within the limits of the ABM Treaty (strictly interpreted) and joined with an arms control policy pursuing deep cuts in offensive weapons. Changing the commonly used

---

[31] Ibid., p. 2.

metaphor, the Aspen Report sees SDI not as a "bargaining chip" but a "lever": "SDI will not likely drive the Soviets to accept offensive reductions that leave asymmetries in our favor. . . . But what SDI can do--and, arguably, hás done in light of the Reykjavik summit--is to prompt the Soviets to offer reductions of a magnitude that eluded U.S. negotiators throughout the 1970s and early 1980s."[32] The wise use of the lever, argues the report, is to strike *The Grand Compromise* of Soviet cuts in their most menacing offensive systems for U.S. restraints--within the ABM Treaty--on defensive technologies.

94. Similar policy perspectives to the Aspen Study are found in the 1985 report of the Stanford Center for International Security and Arms Control, "Strategic Missile Defense: Necessities, Prospects and Dangers in the Near Term."[33] The report is signed by scientists with a wide variety of views on the policy issues of SDI. But supporters and critics of SDI join in recommending research conducted within the parameters of the ABM Treaty, and research which is not pushed by political objectives, but governed by scientific criteria.

95. The purpose in setting forth administration positions and these reports is not to count or even to weigh authorities on the feasibility and arms control issues, but to illustrate how the SDI debate is being joined.

---

[32] Aspen Strategy Group Report, p. 45.

[33] Center for International Security and Arms Control, *Strategic Missile Defense: Necessities, Prospects and Dangers in the Near Term* (Stanford: Stanford University, 1985).

3. SDI: The Moral Argument

96. One of the characteristics of the nuclear debate of the 1980s, fostered in part by *The Challenge of Peace*, has been a growing dissatisfaction with the theory and policy of deterrence. The standard doctrine has come under critique from the left and the right of the political spectrum and both have resorted to moral as well as political-strategic arguments to stress the shortcomings of deterrence. The moral case propounded for defensive systems fits into this wider atmosphere of dissatisfaction with deterrence. Both President Reagan and former Secretary Weinberger regularly appeal to the moral motivation and moral quality of the SDI. Supporters of the SDI pick up on this theme, joining a critique of Mutual Assured Destruction theories to an argument about the moral stability which will accompany a defense dominated nuclear relationship.

97. As bishops, we are interested in the scientific and strategic dimensions of the SDI policy debate, but we are not in a position to contribute to them. It is precisely the visible role which the moral argument has assumed in the policy arena which draws us into more specific commentary here. The SDI is proposed by some of its supporters as a superior moral answer to the moral dilemmas of the nuclear age analyzed in *The Challenge of Peace*. We seek here to probe the relationship of the moral claims made for SDI and other dimensions of the policy debate.

98. The case made for the moral superiority of SDI is primarily an ethic of intention; using the just-war ethic, supporters of SDI review the nuclear age, pointing out how classical deterrence doctrine

has been willing to abide or endorse threats against innocent populations. In contrast to this posture, a case is made describing the *intended objectives* of SDI: either the transition to a world where the nuclear threat has been negated or at least to a world where the principal targets shift from populations to weapons. Stated at the level of intentionality, the SDI case seeks to capture the moral high ground, undoubtedly contributing to the popularity of the program with the general public.

99. But the complexity and the stakes of the policy debate on SDI require that the moral argument be pressed beyond its intended objectives. The SDI debate is less a dispute about objectives or motives than it is about means and consequences. To probe the moral content of the effects of pursuing SDI is to raise issues about its risks, costs and benefits.

100. Giving proper weight to the effects of pursuing SDI moves the focus of the moral argument back from the desirability of freeing the world from the *factual condition* of an assured destruction posture (an objective commended by everyone) to the *technological feasibility* of fulfilling this intention, to the potential risks for *strategic stability* of an offensive-defensive arms competition and to the *economic costs* and *trade-offs* which pursuit of SDI will require in a deficit-ridden federal budget. These categories of feasibility, stability and cost are already prominent in the SDI debate. The point here is to assert that the moral character of SDI cannot be determined apart from these other elements precisely because consequences count in a moral assessment.

101. First, while the feasibility argument is primarily a scientific-technological question, there

are risks associated with pursuing some technological paths:

- risks to the existing arms control regime;
- risks of introducing dimensions of uncertainty into the already delicate political-psychological fabric of deterrence;
- risks that defensive systems can have real or perceived offensive uses;
- finally, risks that some forms of SDI would be ineffective against an adversary's first-strike, but more effective against a retaliatory second-strike, thereby eroding crisis stability.

Assessing these risks--evaluating which are prudent to pursue, which are too high to tolerate--involves a moral as well as a technological judgment. Precisely because of the number and quality of scientific judgments which have warned against precipitous movement toward SDI, it is necessary to stress the need for continued technological scrutiny and moral restraint concerning a decision which might later be regretted.

102. The second question concerns the impact of the defensive option on strategic stability. The critics of deterrence (*The Challenge of Peace* included) detail several negative factors in the deterrence regime, but the judgments of Vatican II, Pope John Paul II and the pastoral letter also posit a role for deterrence in a world of sovereign states armed with nuclear weapons. While the need to move "beyond deterrence" is asserted by both Pope John Paul II and the U.S. bishops, there is also found in their statements the logic of the 1976 Vatican statement at the United Nations: that a

move beyond deterrence should not place the world in a more dangerous condition than our present plight.[34] Hence, moves beyond deterrence are open to scrutiny. They must be assessed in light of their impact on the basic purpose of deterrence--its role in preventing the use of nuclear weapons.

103. Assessment of SDI in light of its impact on strategic stability will force the moral argument onto the path of examining the contrasting views of whether the "transition" from assured destruction to common security can be carried off with acceptable risk. Supporters of the SDI argue from the moral and the strategic perspective about the opportunities it provides to transform the nuclear dilemma--to end the mutual threats which constitute the present delicate deterrence balance.[35] These arguments stress the goal of the transition.

104. While this goal is undoubtedly attractive, the more compelling moral case presently rests with those who specify the likely risks of an aggressive SDI program at this time:

1. the obstacle it poses to effective movement on arms control;
2. the possible shift toward offensive use of this defensive system;

---

[34] "Statement of the Holy See to the United Nations General Assembly," *L'Osservatore Romano,* English weekly edition (June 17, 1976): p. 9.

[35] Cf. K.B. Payne and C. Gray, "Nuclear Policy and the Defensive Transition," *Foreign Affairs* 62:4 (1984): pp. 820-842; G. Weigel, "Breaking the Doctrinal Gridlock: Common Security and the Strategic Defensive Initiative," *This World* 16 (Winter 1987): pp. 3-22.

3. the further "tilt" of the deterrence relationship toward preemptive strategies during the transition period.

No one of these results is a certain consequence of pursuing SDI deployment but the collective danger they pose to the dynamic of deterrence leaves us unconvinced of the merits of proceeding toward deployment of the system. The combination of the technological and the strategic evaluations of the present status of SDI appear to us to promise serious risks and very hypothetical benefits at this time.

105. The feasibility and strategic stability arguments are central to the policy debate about SDI. Third, the economic argument--the escalating cost of SDI in a time of continuing budget deficits and in a decade which has seen deep cuts in programs for the poor at home and abroad--has particular moral relevance. While *The Challenge of Peace* recognized the need for and moral legitimacy of defense spending, it followed recent papal and conciliar teaching in pressing for limits on military spending. The deep divisions in the technological community about the feasibility of SDI, the arguments cited above about the negative impact on strategic stability and the certainty of the costs of SDI bring it within the framework of the Bernardin-O'Connor criteria cited earlier in this report. Specifically, their judgment is that a program which fails to attract a clear consensus on technological-strategic grounds should not be allowed to command resources at a time when other human needs go unfulfilled.

106. In summary, our primary purpose in this section has been to dispel the notion that the moral character of SDI can be decided simply by examining it in terms of the objectives (or ends that

it intends). These are not the only morally relevant factors that need to be taken into account in rendering a moral judgment about SDI. Judged within an adequate moral framework, one that takes into account the relevant moral circumstances surrounding this policy, it is our prudential judgment that proposals to press deployment of SDI do not measure up to the moral criteria outlined in this report. Our judgment about SDI can be summarized in the following statements:

1. Some of the officially stated objectives of the SDI program, to move away from a long-term reliance on deterrence and to protect civilians and society as a whole, correspond to key themes of the pastoral letter.

2. The pursuit of these objectives must be carried out within limits which protect other principles of the pastoral letter:
   a) that the framework of arms control agreements and negotiations not be eroded or made more difficult;
   b) that a new surge of offensive competition not be stimulated as a consequence of introducing defensive proposals;
   c) that the stability of deterrence not be weakened in an untested attempt to transcend or enhance it;
   d) that defense spending as a whole not absorb a morally disproportionate percentage of the federal budget.

3. Observing these limits in the immediate future requires that:
   a) SDI be maintained as a research and development program, within the

restraints of the ABM Treaty, not
pressed to deployment;

b) the ABM Treaty should not be cast
aside or overridden;

c) a specific test of each new step in SDI
be an assessment of its effects on the
offensive-defensive interaction of
the arms competition;

d) clear criteria be established about
spending for SDI in relationship to
other needs in legitimate defense expenditures (e.g., conventional forces)
and particularly in relationship to
the basic human needs of the poor in
our country and in other nations.

C. The Economy and Military Spending

107. The last criterion for SDI actually must be
applied to the entire range of military spending. A
persistent theme in the papal and conciliar
teaching on peace is the need to redirect national
and global resources from arms to human and social
development objectives. From the classic statement
of Vatican II--"the arms race is an utterly
treacherous trap for humanity, and one which
injures the poor to an intolerable degree"[36]--to the
repeated statements of John Paul II on the same
theme, the imperative to contain military
spending and increase aid to the poor is stated with
utter clarity. The same utter clarity marks the

---

[36] *Gaudium et Spes (Pastoral Constitution on the
Church in the Modern World)*, no. 81. Published in
W.M. Abbott, SJ, ed., *The Documents of Vatican II* (New
York: The America Press, 1966).

record of recent military spending--the moral imperative is being ignored or violated. A 1986 U.N. Declaration on Disarmament and Development by a panel of distinguished experts tells the sorry story: "In over four decades since the establishment of the United Nations, the worldwide military spending has rarely fallen in real terms during any period of time. The current military expenditures represent well over 5 per cent of total world output and are over 25 times as large as all official development assistance to developing countries."[37]

108. While many nations, including developing countries, drive the trend of military spending, the U.N. Declaration correctly observes that "[t]he bulk of global military spending remains concentrated among the industrialized countries . . . ."[38] Among the industrialized nations, the superpowers lead the way. This pattern of increasing investment in the arms competition in light of the global disparities of wealth and poverty was criticized in both the peace and economic pastoral letters. The pattern is morally unacceptable. No one has more persistently argued the moral case for reallocation of global resources than Pope John Paul II. In *On Social Concern* he reiterated a theme which has characterized his pontificate:

> The first consideration of the striking content of the Encyclical's historic phrase may be supplemented by a second

[37] Abdel-Rahman, et al., *Disarmament and Development: Joint Declaration by the Panel of Eminent Personalities in the Field of Disarmament and Development* (New York, United Nations, 1986): p. 1.
[38] Ibid.

consideration to which the document itself alludes: how can one justify the fact that *huge sums of money*, which could and should be used for increasing the development of peoples, are instead utilized for the enrichment of individuals or groups, or assigned to the increase of stockpiles of weapons, both in developed countries and in the developing ones, thereby upsetting the real priorities? This is even more serious given the difficulties which often hinder the direct transfer of capital set aside for helping needy countries. If "development is the new name for peace," war and military preparations are the major enemy of the integral development of peoples (no. 10).

109. The 1980s version of defense versus social spending took on new dimensions of tension within the United States as social programs for the poor were cut and as federal budget deficits (the product to a great extent of high military spending and tax cuts) grew to destabilizing proportions. Since the publication of *The Challenge of Peace*, the pastoral on the economy, *Economic Justice for All*,[39] has focused attention on the persistence of poverty within the United States. The budget debate each year makes clear that a direct and unyielding competition exists between defense and social spending. Social spending covers federal expenditures for health care, housing, food and

[39] National Conference of Catholic Bishops, *Economic Justice For All: Pastoral Letter on Catholic Social Teaching and the U.S. Economy* (Washington, D.C.: USCC Office of Publishing and Promotion Services, 1986).

nutrition and income security for children and families classified as poor. These specific areas of health, nutrition and housing for the poor were precisely the concerns of *Economic Justice for All.*[40]

110. We do not think the determination of a just level of defense expenditures is a simple task. We know the cheapest defense is often an increasingly nuclear defense. To avoid that trend we stated in 1983 that we would consider raising expenditures for conventional forces if this decreased the nuclear danger. We still are prepared, in light of the pastoral letter and the Bernardin-O'Connor criteria, to assess programs on their merits. But it is clear that our two pastoral letters point toward the need to reduce defense spending in the 1980s as a percentage of our national budget, to test scrupulously programs certain to consume large revenues and to recognize that national and international security can be threatened by causes other than military forces.

III. The Status of Deterrence
An Evaluation

111. The judgment of "strictly conditioned moral acceptance" of deterrence in 1983 was meant to convey the strategic paradox and moral problem we encountered in evaluating nuclear policy. The essential moral question, defined above, remains: Can credible deterrence be reconciled with right intention, proportionality and discrimination?

---

[40] Cf. ibid., nos. 136-292.

112. In 1983, we were not persuaded to condemn deterrence, nor were we prepared simply to endorse it. Its contribution to peace is the paradoxical role it plays in restraining the use of nuclear weapons. We could not disprove this claim, and we found some reasons to be convinced by it. At the same time, the negative dimensions of the deterrence relationship--its danger, its costs, its capacity to perpetuate divisions in international affairs--were there for all to see. Hence, the *most* we could say in support of deterrence was "conditional acceptance."

113. Since *The Challenge of Peace* was published, the ethical commentary on it and on the problem of nuclear deterrence has been voluminous. The statements of other episcopal conferences, the declarations of other churches and religious organizations, the writings of philosophers, statesmen and political analysts have all grappled with the moral status of deterrence policy.

114. It is possible to sketch the broad outlines of this commentary. Some, using the principles of discrimination and proportionality, as we did, believe that emerging technology in the nuclear field (increasing accuracy and miniaturization of warheads) will provide a deterrent force which is both strategically credible and morally justifiable. When this technological faith is combined with a certain definition of the threat facing the West, it seems to provide for its supporters a coherent moral theory of deterrence. Nuclear threat and even use are a proportionate response to the political threat faced by the West, and the new technology

provides a legitimate means to use if deterrence fails.[41]

115. A very different analysis of the nuclear relationship finds justification of deterrence policy--even conditional acceptance--a mistaken view of what exists. In this moral assessment, deterrence policy is inherently tied to a willingness to go to countersociety warfare, bursting all the moral bonds needed to keep warfare within the moral universe. This reading of the nuclear reality finds no grounds for any acceptance of the existing strategy of deterrence.[42]

116. These choices, and variants of them, were before us when we wrote *The Challenge of Peace.* Our answer to the moral dilemma of deterrence policy, then and now, is less clear-cut than either of these positions. In trying to address all the factors of the deterrence relationship--including the values served by it and those threatened by it-- it has seemed to us a problem where absolute clarity in one answer often sacrifices part of the problem to be solved. Our judgment is not as confident about technology as the first view, or as convinced about the intrinsic evil of nuclear deterrence, taken as a whole, as the second view.

117. Deterrence, of course, is not an entity but a policy. It is a policy involving several component

---

[41] See, e.g., A. Wohlstetter, "Bishops, Statesmen, and Other Strategists on the Bombing of Innocents," *Commentary* (June 1983): pp. 15-35; report of the Commission on Integrated Long-Term Strategy, *Discriminate Deterrence* (Washington, D.C.: January 1988).

[42] See, e.g., J. Finnis, J.M. Boyle, Jr. and G. Grisez, *Nuclear Deterrence, Morality and Realism* (Oxford: Clarendon Press, 1987).

elements: weapons systems, force posture, declaratory policy, targeting doctrine and the relationship of these to the objectives of security policy and--an aspect of it--arms control policy. As others have noted, when one looks back on the evolution of the nuclear age, it is highly unlikely that anyone would have chosen to have our present situation result. The deterrence relationship has been shaped by many forces, not all of them coherently related to each other.

118. Yet, any assessment of the policy of deterrence will be hard-put not to acknowledge that in a world of widespread nuclear knowledge and at least six nuclear powers, deterrence has been a significant factor in preventing the use of nuclear weapons. This attribute of deterrence weighed heavily with us in the writing of *The Challenge of Peace* and it does so now. Beyond this fundamental function, nuclear deterrence most likely has contributed to a more cautious posture of the two nuclear powers in world affairs.

119. But this side of the nuclear equation must be balanced against the various costs of nuclear deterrence. The political cost of two powers holding the fate of the northern hemisphere (and probably much of the south too) hostage is clearly an unacceptable way to structure international relations. Even the caution of superpowers is not immune from criticism, since they have found ways to engage each other through proxy forces in other nations, often at the expense of the latter. Pope John Paul II spoke directly to this reality in *On Social Concern:*

> International relations, in turn, could not fail to feel the effects of this "logic of the blocs" and of the respective "spheres of

influence." The tension between the two blocs which began at the end of the Second World War has dominated the whole of the subsequent forty years . . . . In light of these considerations, we easily arrive at a clearer picture of the last twenty years and a better understanding of the conflicts in the northern hemisphere, namely between East and West, as an important cause of the retardation or stagnation of the South (nos. 20, 22).

120. Psychologically, the costs of living with the nuclear threat have been documented in both East and West. Economically, the diversion of resources over the long-term to the nuclear competition has merited the critique and condemnation of secular and religious leadership. Finally, as we have analyzed above, the deterrence relationship is not static. The technological drive in recent years has moved the competition in directions which erode the stability of deterrence and increase the chance of nuclear use.

121. We remain convinced that the policy of nuclear deterrence is not a stable long-term method of keeping the peace among sovereign states. This is still the foundation of our evaluation of deterrence policy. We are also convinced that in the short-term and midterm assessment of our future the best moral evaluation is neither to condemn deterrence outright nor to accept it as self-regulating or "normal."

122. More precisely, we are persuaded to renew the judgment of *The Challenge of Peace:* that nuclear deterrence merits only strictly conditioned acceptance. In a dangerous world, a world of both widespread nuclear knowledge and extensive

nuclear arsenals, we find condemning nuclear deterrence too drastic a solution and embracing it too simple a response. With Pope John Paul II we hope

> that all countries, and especially the great powers, will perceive more and more that the fear of "assured mutual destruction," which is at the heart of the doctrine of nuclear deterrence, cannot be a reliable basis for security and peace in the long term.[43]

123. This assessment of various elements of deterrence policy is less dramatic than a single univocal judgment, but we believe it is more adequate to the complex pattern of U.S.-Soviet relations which exists today and is most appropriate for us as we call on our own country and other nations to pursue more effectively bilateral and multilateral arms control and to move decisively toward progressive disarmament.

124. Our purpose in writing this report has been to test whether "conditional acceptance" of deterrence continues to define the moral significance of the deterrence relationship. Specifically we have measured the conditions set forth in 1983 against the empirical trends and developments of the past five years. In this examination, we have found some steps commendable and other trends eroding both strategic stability and the legitimacy of deterrence policy. The lack of clear movement in the direction of a more stable deterrent and ultimately disarmament causes us profound concern. We are not satisfied with the progress on these fronts in recent years.

---

[43] John Paul II, "Address to Diplomatic Corps," no. 5, p. 7.

125. Some who follow the judgment of the pastoral letter on the policy of deterrence may conscientiously conclude that present U.S. policy does not meet the strict conditions set forth and that there is no reasonable expectation of significant change in the future. Such persons will obviously oppose that policy. They believe such opposition is the logical consequent of a judgment which gives conditioned moral acceptance to deterrence.

126. Our committee's response is not to drop "conditional acceptance," but to advocate more actively a series of measures which still very much need to be undertaken to meet the conditions of *The Challenge of Peace.* Our "conditional acceptance" is not an endorsement of a status quo that we find inadequate and dangerous. It is a position that requires us to work for genuine and far-reaching changes in the policies that guide nuclear arsenals of the world. More particularly it requires us to continue to pursue and advocate a more secure and morally justifiable basis for peace based on the following criteria:

1. Deterrence based on the direct targeting of urban populations is morally unacceptable. We oppose it in all cases.
2. Deterrence policy implemented by weapons which combine size, accuracy and multiple warheads in a credible "first-strike" posture adds unacceptable risk to the deterrence relationship. We, therefore, oppose existing trends and will oppose future policies, which push the deterrence posture of both superpowers in this direction.

3. The dynamic of the existing policies of both superpowers enhances the risk of the preemptive use of nuclear weapons. We advocate reversal of this process as the first goal of arms control policy.

4. The levels of strategic armaments far exceed the requirements of survivable second-strike deterrence--the only posture to which conditional acceptance can be given. We support "deep cuts" in strategic forces as the second goal of arms control policy.

5. The risks of provoking an offensive and defensive competition between the superpowers and the existing disparity of views about the nature, purpose and feasibility of space-based defense are more compelling to us than the promises made about the program. We oppose anything beyond a well-defined research and development program clearly within the restraints of the ABM Treaty.

6. Our acceptance of deterrence is conditioned upon serious efforts at restraining proliferation. Existing policies of the superpowers are clearly inadequate on this question. We urge a renewed effort in the coming decade to halt the spread of nuclear weapons.

7. The first major nuclear arms control treaty was a partial ban on testing. Twenty-five years later the U.S. and Soviet Union, along with the other nuclear states, have failed to fulfill the promise of that first step. We call for a renewed effort, pursued with much greater purpose and conviction, to complete

negotiations on a comprehensive test ban treaty. We call for ratification of both the Threshold Test Ban Treaty and the Peaceful Nuclear Explosions Treaty.

8. The competition in nonnuclear arms must also be addressed. We urge more concerted efforts to outlaw the production, possession and use of chemical and biological weapons and to reduce conventional forces to a new balance compatible with reasonable requirements for defense.

9. The cost of the arms competition is a continuing indictment of its role in international politics. The distortions in resource allocation by the superpowers and other nations--large and small, rich and poor--fit Pope John Paul's description of "a structure of sin." He rightly describes present global patterns of military spending as a process leading toward death rather than development.[44] We will support efforts to redirect budgetary choices in the United States toward greater attention to the poor at home and abroad.

127. The conditions just specified are aimed at containing the nuclear competition, reducing its risks, enhancing chances for arms reduction and ultimately using arms control as a step toward nuclear disarmament. These measures were central to *The Challenge of Peace* and this report seeks to

[44] *On Social Concern,* no. 24. For the most recent statistics on military spending and social spending see, e.g., R.L. Sivard, *World Military and Social Expenditures 1987-88* (Washington, D.C.: 1988) 12th edition.

update and refine our recommendations for reducing dangers of the nuclear age. The challenge was stated clearly and urgently in the message of Pope John Paul II delivered by Cardinal Casaroli to the United Nations Third Special Session on Disarmament:

> Disarmament is not an end in itself. The end is peace, and security is one of its essential elements. The evolution of international relations today reveals that disarmament is a necessary condition, if not the primary condition, for security . . . . [T]he type of security on which our planet has depended for the last several decades--a balance of terror based on nuclear deterrence--is a security with a far too high risk level. This awareness should encourage Nations to enter into a new phase in their relations with all due urgency.[45]

128. This report is written at a time when a complementary strategy must be pressed. We are skeptical about escaping the strategic and moral dilemmas of the nuclear age through technology (either in space or by more accurate weapons). The complementary strategy which needs to be pressed is a creative and sustained effort to reshape the political dimension of U.S.-Soviet relations. Such an effort should seek to relativize the nuclear component of this relationship. This is an enormously complex process--tried often before with few positive results. But it is worth another effort, not only to lessen the danger of a superpower

---

[45] John Paul II, "Message to Third U.N. Special Session on Disarmament" (New York, June 2, 1988), *Origins* 18:5 (June 16, 1988): no. 2, p. 67.

confrontation but also to limit the ways in which present East-West competition is injected into the conflicts of others, transforming them into ever more intractable problems.

129. To contain the nuclear danger of our time is itself an awesome undertaking. To reshape the political fabric of an increasingly interdependent world is an even larger and more complicated challenge. But it is precisely this possibility which engages the interest of both political analysts and religious and moral thinkers in our day. It is this question of fashioning the future of relationships among states and peoples that Pope John Paul II addressed in *On Social Concern*. The call of the encyclical to go beyond "the logic of the blocs" is addressed in a particular fashion to the U.S. and the Soviet Union, but the concern of the letter reaches beyond the superpower competition to the needs of the vast majority of the globe who are affected by the superpower competition but are not capable of influencing it:

> Surmounting every type of *imperialism* and determination to preserve their *own hegemony*, the stronger and richer nations must have a sense of moral *responsibility* for the other nations, so that a *real international system* may be established which will rest on the foundation of the *equality* of all peoples and on the necessary respect for their legitimate differences. The economically weaker countries, or those still at subsistence level, must be enabled, with the assistance of other peoples and of the international community, to make a contribution of their own to the common good with their treasures of

humanity and *culture*, which otherwise would be lost for ever (no. 39).

130. This is a call to fundamental change in the pattern of international politics. Such fundamental changes do not occur easily or quickly in the life of states and nations. They are the product of both deep historical forces and intelligent, courageous human choices. Success in these endeavors is never assured and progress is maintained only by continual effort and initiative. But changes do occur. In the West the seventeenth century marked the end of large scale religious wars and the twentieth century--after two major wars--has a record of sustained peace among the democracies.

131. The cosmic challenge of the papal encyclical to go beyond "the logic of the blocs" in the name of both keeping the nuclear peace and building the peace through just relations with the poor of the world is larger in scope and more complex in substance than either of the successes noted above. But nothing less than this kind of vision--joining the East-West issues and the North-South issues in a coherent plan--is equal to the world in which we live.

132. We are convinced that the present time is better served by those willing to risk falling short of a large vision than the alternative risk of being satisfied with small achievements which fail to address the dangers or the opportunities of the moment. In that spirit we submit this report on the meaning of *The Challenge of Peace* in 1988.